When Mashiach Comes

By Ruby M. Grossblatt; Illustrated by Aaron Friedman

Dedicated in memory of my beloved parents,
George and Sylvia Kasten ע"ה

When Mashiach comes will I be standing in my Pesach outfit at the start of our *seder*?

Or will I be peeking into the newly scrubbed kitchen cabinets searching for the *afikoman*?

Will I be roasting potatoes at a Lag B'Omer bonfire?

Or will I be counting the last few days of the *Omer* hoping that I don't miss a night?

When Mashiach comes will I be learning Torah with my friends late Shavuos night?

Or will I be eating creamy cherry cheesecake at lunch?

Will I be sitting on the carpeted floor as I hear Jeremiah's words of sadness?

Or will I be sweeping the kitchen floor with Ima on Tisha B'Av afternoon?

When Mashiach comes will I be shaping smooth, round raisin *challahs* for Rosh Hashanah?

Or will I be dipping an apple into honey hoping that Hashem will "give us a good, sweet year"?

Will I be calling my best friend during the Ten Days of Repentance? "Chaim, do you forgive me for anything I did that hurt you?"

Or will I be fasting half a day on Yom Kippur, begging Hashem to accept our prayers?

When Mashiach comes will I be standing in the *succah* beside Ima as she lights the candles?

Or will I be sitting under the canopy of pine needles watching the stars shine through?

Will I be listening to the Torah reading on Simchas Torah, then dancing and waving my flag?

Or will I be holding my little brother's hand as we hurry under the huge cover of *talisos*?

When Mashiach comes will I be lighting a *menorah* singing *Maoz Tzur*...?

Or will I be watching a *dreidel* spin round and round hoping it will land on *gimmel*!

Will Chaim and I be shaking our *groggers* loudly on Purim, drowning out the name of Haman?

Or will Chani be delivering *shalach manos* baskets to our neighbors, a silver Queen Esther crown on her head?

When Mashiach comes will I be holding the *Havdalah* candle high?

Or will I be smelling the sweet chocolate cake as Ima serves *Melaveh Malkah*?

When Mashiach comes will I be running around the playground at recess with Masha, my friend from Russia?

Or will I be saying *Shema* with my little sister Dini in bed at night — or *Modeh Ani* in the morning, pushing off the warm covers to start a new day?

We don't know when Mashiach will come, but we can help him hurry. By doing mitzvos every day.

And when he finally comes...

...the whole world will be doing mitzvos too. We're ready! Are you?!

Glossary

afikoman: piece of matzah eaten as dessert at the ***Pesach*** seder
challahs: bread served at festive meals
dreidel: spinning top used on ***Chanuka***
gimmel: the "winning" letter on the ***dreidel***
grogger: noisemaker used on ***Purim***
Havdalah: prayer recited at the conclusion of Sabbath
Lag B'Omer: minor holiday between ***Pesach*** and ***Shavuos***
Maoz Tzur: Chanukah song
Melaveh Malkah: meal served after Sabbath
Menorah: Candelabrum used for ***Chanukah***
Modeh Ani: prayer recited upon awakening in themorning
Omer: forty-nine-day period between ***Pesach*** and ***Shavuos***
Pesach: Passover
Purim: merry holiday celebrating the downfall of Haman
Rosh Hashanah: Jewish New Year
seder: service of ***Pesach*** night
shalach manos: gifts sent to friends on ***Purim***
Shavuos: holiday commemorating the giving of the Torah
Shema: bedtime prayer
Simchas Torah: Holiday of Rejoicing with the Torah
succah: hut used for meals during the holiday of ***Succos***
talisos: (pl.) prayer shawls
Tisha B'Av: day of mourning commemorating the destruction of the Temple
Yom Kippur: Day of Atonement